I subside by the seaside.

AF624812

Asheda Weekes

BookLeaf Publishing

Presentation by *BookLeaf Publishing*

Web: www.bookleafpub.com

E-mail: info@bookleafpub.com

ISBN: 9789357445610

First edition 2022

DEDICATION

To Travers & Erin, for the unwavering support as I return back to the words.

And Kata, for oceans can't break the ties that bind us. I miss you.

ACKNOWLEDGEMENT

To Jacqui Norman for a collaborative imagination and creating the cover design.

And my mother for being an enigmatic energy of inspiration.

I acknowledge the traditional owners and custodians of the land on which I write. I pay respects to elders past, present, and emerging and recognise their continuing connection to land, waterways, and community. Sovereignty has never been ceded. It always was and always will be, Aboriginal land.

PREFACE

Sometimes I can hear my bones straining under the weight of all the lives I'm not living.

— Jonathan Safran Foer, Extremely Loud & Incredibly Close

I subside by the seaside.

I subside by the seaside
collapsed at the grain —
self in sand and
salvaging the grace of
misguided solace.

we're running parallel. (2016)

we're running parallel,
unable to reach
but held in such fitted alignment.
(when fully thought)

and the sight has kept
all my loving in a constant
consistent
change of balance.

edge of illusion,
a doubted misconception
that keeps us,
that builds (us) a stop
but
moves us
in such an immaculate
moment.

if you've been pulled in (I)

I.
if you've been pulled in,
I assure you that line pierced from touch
and frayed into your arteries
straight up—an attack on the heart
a brush up on the skin.

if you've been pulled in (II-IV)

II.
you’ve sunken in,
lingering lines pierced from
soft-touch & stolen glances
an energy of undeniable
lust(re)
of undeni— an attack on
the heart/ breathless wonder

III.
time has surpassed and
distance settles… you.
dormant energy residual
tapered on my arteries
withdrawing air from my lungs into
absolute euphoria.

IV.
burst and pulled in (again)
rippling through my veins.

full circle at 27.

Twenty-seven years ago
My mother was twenty-seven years old.
She tasted the cool dry air,
Foreign to her brown skin.

She made a home between Fawkner and Tan
A polished subversion from the
Jalan-jalan of KLC and Kuching.

And as her belly grew,
Strangeness subsided.
The fondness settled in.
She swapped a waddled walk,
For a stroller and wide-eyed
China doll. *(Beloved)*.

Years between she built
A family setting roots
In a transcontinental cosmopolitan space.
Cold dust to subservient humidity
Before finding permanence
On Gunaikurnai Land.

But twenty-seven years later
A few roads down the way,

I step out daily on the streets.
Between Fawkner and Tan
As the twenty-seven-year-old daughter
Making a home in the same space
Wrapped in the memory of hers.

Vantablack.

I've been told the black energy
I carry beneath my skin
radiates the ebb of panic
that I so deeply fixate on
masking.

A distant relative, a medium of sorts
told my mother
She has a dark cloud over her head,
the air she breathes is polluted
I was only thirteen.

Most days I want to fold into myself
a fifteen year-old
that read books all-day
and had more confidence
then this body that's aged ten more years.

restless, rumination

the backlog of thought
shifts in rudimentary
restless rumination
a catalogue lost in
unwritten paces
revolving in indecision
how do you unpack
a decade worth of whispers (?) and
stolen glances
of forged mindlessness
than the promising transaction
of reflective reprehension
indulgent revelation
lost in the foray
and lustre of solaced
written comprehension

for optimal results (I)

For optimal results
Wake — with the sun
twist the spine, stretch the limbs
pair a concoction of daily vitamins and medications
with a glass of (lemon?) water
take three deep breaths, or a
guided meditation.

Move — daily for thirty-minutes
ten-thousand steps or a variation
stretch, flow, lift and pulsate
to wake the muscle
aid the joints
feel the heart.
With at least forty kegels daily
for a strong pelvic floor.

Wash — the body head to toe
lather up armpits, crotch and feet
every second day —
massage shampoo into the scalp
rinse and repeat from root to tip
condition for two minutes
upgrade to a spa experience
dry brush to body scrub twice a week

move gently in circular motions
at least three minutes.

Teeth — cleaning requires attention
two minute thirty seconds each quadrant
a dollop of toothpaste spread into foam
from side to side, up and down, near the gum
twice daily.
twice. daily.
floss crevasses of teeth in patient rhythm
a thread of one point five feet each time.
daily.
See the dentist every six months.

for optimal results (II)

For optimal results
Body — lotion applied daily
ample pumps spread thick on the skin and
rubbed into translucency
*Hot tip: the back of your hand can reach
your shoulder blades*
deodorise as needed,
especially summer thighs and cracks
option to spritz a ~~fruity~~ / *floral* / herbaceous scent
a waft from the wrist and neck.

Cleanse — the face for sixty seconds
Gently massage, rinse then before pat-dry
the pump of serum, tone, moisturise
(gua sha optional) and
two-fingers length of SPF*
**Reapply every three hours.*
twice or thrice a week, indulge in a twenty-minute
fac—eye— lip mask?
for a perfect dewy finish.
*Ps. All skincare to be used within twelve
months of opening*

Hair — styling interchanges
thick, thin, straight or curly,

blow-dry, heat, coloured, up, down, with bangs
sprays, creams and pastes to make it
look effortless, look natural, look fun.
(please micro clean your hairbrush).
Ask your hairdresser*
**see them every four to six weeks*

Make — up the face
Brows, eyes and lashes
Foundation, concealer, blush, bronzer etc etc
A fun lipstick or lip —
Does it really matter with this
perpetuating mask-wearing?
<u>*Ps. All make-up to be used within twelve months of opening...*</u>
<u>*That's three months for mascara.*</u>

Dress — to weather
To comfort, to work appropriation
Change underwear daily
(or after a sweaty workout)
Clasp a fresh bra every three wears
Shirts, blouses, pants or slacks every two-to-three*
Jeans every six weeks*
Spot clean as needed.
(Read material labels to avoid disappointment)
**pending fabric and quality*

for optimal results (III)

Between —
pack essentia—*keys-wallet-lipstick-headphones etc.*
eat breakfast
make lunch
be earlier rather than later
do the demands of your day-to-day job but also
Attend Meetings! Workshop! Water cooler talk!
Network! Professional development!
        smile to strangers.
see your friends
call your grandmother
pay the bills
water and rotate your plants as required per-
clean the house to the frequency of each shore
"refrigerate after opening."
        consume within two to three days
play with your pet
play with your kids
keep up with pop culture
keep up with politics
keep up with the world
participate in pop culture / politics / the world
have a hobby
have a side hustle
<u>relax</u>.   relax.   *relax*.

for optimal results (IV)

Beau— to gratify your own needs
tan daily, weekly or once-off
gel manicure every three weeks
laminate brows every four to six weeks
lash lift and tint every six to eight weeks
facial remedies three to four weeks
laser hair removal four to six weeks
botox every three months
**space out accordingly to events, exercise, sex and showers*

for optimal results (V)

For optimal results
read — a book for thirty minutes
watch — *any screen* two hours no more
listen — to music for seventy-eight minutes
breathe — nature for two hours
drink — eight glasses of water a day
eat — five servings of veg and two pieces of fruit
enjoy —two twenty-five to three twenty-five
grams of carbs.
hug— another eight to twelve times daily or
touch — eight meaningful times; hand-holding,
kisses, pats on backs, and high-fives
stand — up every thirty minutes for thirty minutes
sleep — for seven to nine hours each night*
no screens thirty minutes before bed*
*** a perfect amount of time to read.*

for optimal results (VI)

For optimal results
don't forget to
BSE (breast self-exam) monthly
check skin and moles quarterly
have routine blood draw & eyes checked yearly
pap smear every three years
etc. etc.   *etc.* *
**changes pending on age*

see a therapist as needed for:
general health, sex health, mental health, chronic condition, sore joints, energy
on ebbs and flows of weekly to monthly and
the condition to the rule in between.

for optimal results (VII)

Undress — the day's demands
swap comfort for *le plus de* comfort.
pull the socks off sweating feet
and claustrophobic breasts.

Move? — wash?
make — down the face
double-cleanse sixty seconds around
repeat a tweaked sun salutation routine

night serums, oils and heavy creams
in sequential of every surface
face, body, hands and feet.
teeth, hair and crevasses in between.

Pour— the red or peppermint tea
and light the candles
wind down to the hum and
journal the dark corners of your mind
the highlight reels of unrequited ambition.

Doze— off in eighteen degrees
repeat the wake in reverse to
the sounds of the seaside

brushing on the cliff
weights of blankets grounding
for *optimal* sense of being.

on read.

set boundaries in (allotted) time
for the expectation of communication
tailored to each connection
demanding its own set of etiquette—
forty-eight hours to respond
a day to turnaround
hours to reply
minutes to be *on read*
seconds to tie sentences together
milliseconds to fracture attentio—

reply weeks later.

I've etched a halo of skin.

I’ve etched a halo of skin
Three inches wider than
My fluctuating state.

I’ll bruise to the bone or
Suck my belly into
Elastic constriction
And still be
Three inches more
Of an invisible monster surrounding me.

I lack

I lack
humour
a backbone to not shed tears
the impromptu plan
or non-punitive disappointment
a left of centre trend
of nonchalan—t(wist your arm for attention)
an immediate glass half full mentality.
shattered confidence to the bone
please don't make a joke on my lack thereof
it's grating. really.

but I am

but I am the immediacy—
the thought of breakfast made
caffeine wafting through the air
the tug of the shirt at night
a care package dropped off
a lovenote in any form
the understated message of *I miss you.*
            the indulgence in finding the perfect gift
for the perfect person
a rare laughter at undetermined humour
to be of unfaltering eyes and shy smiles
to unpack secrets within minutes
and move with you on the dancefloor
            (I'll take the shots if you insist)
a whisper of twofold sadness
a holding of hands in the moonlight
and fondness held in loss, forgotten, collapsed
the ache for permeating glows.

Papaveroideae

Stems round and lift
Soft zig-zags of heightened
blasé perfection.
Like weeds or daddy-long-legs
a non-binary elegance
from bud to bloom—
venus fly traps clam
bright petals that concave
in warm illumination
a slowness in bloom
where disintegration is just a beautiful
no wilt
no sadness
zig-zags in perfect composition
just petals and pollen fallen
in candid disarray.

locked down.

I.
Lockdown
an unprecedented
cataclysmic
small waft of excitement
optimising work-from-home freedom
naivety of 'this will be over soon*
**soon: six to eight weeks tops.*

II.
Lockdown
after a stint at reconnection
the longest winter stretched
between masked curfews
and coffee walks
the itch then agitation
of one-hundred-and-twelve days
fogginess and restlessness
in a paralysing yearn for
lost time.

III.
Lockdown

a snap back into
a subdued trauma
'you know the drill'
resilience is paramount but
grieve as you need.
folding into temporary
short-term
success?*
**?— surreal lingers.*

IV.
Lockdown
another snap
accumulating heat
loss of life, life lived, livelihood, life milestones
trauma subsides in shock—
a delayed acceptance
it's been a year since soon never happened.

V.
Lockdown
snap extended (again)
the art of planning subverted
a city revival collapsing
on cancellations
and TBCs.
(one more)

VI.
Lockd—well fuck this

rinse and repeat
the pattern of delayed shock reactions
the lack of pla—
the lack of desire to plan
bellowing the unwillingness
to get out of bed
            there's no time for lockd—hobbies, side
hustles <u>etc.</u> etc.   *etc.*
when you're too tired to
practice the basic necessities
for optimal results
too tired from symptomatic
            the world is on fire.

VII. Lockdown
post — the edge is near
unsettling reverb to
the new normal
out of shells for :
            face-to-face interaction
a horror of a shameful cough
a closeness beyond one point five metres
masks on condition.
with an itch to plan
cautious in exhilaration
to hit play from the pause
of a locked down intermission.

bouy on the coastline.

bouy on the coastline
is a squint of bright orange—
that's where you'll find me upon the current
afloat against seaside cliffs
surrendering to the grain
sweltering at the surface
sometimes basking in clear skies
a bobble in the sun.
above the ebb and
beyond the flow
salvaging the grace
of solace on the seaside.

www.ingramcontent.com/pod-product-compliance
Lightning Source LLC
Chambersburg PA
CBHW051752130826
49812CB00033B/1110
* 9 7 8 9 3 5 7 4 4 5 6 1 0 *